Vivek Achary



# DM 101

## DIGITAL MARKETING 101

How to sell stuff without selling your soul

First Edition: 2017
Second Edition: 2025
Printed in India

Printed at Trinity Academy, Mumbai
Typeset in Adobe Garamond Pro

ISBN: 978-93-6070-188-8

Cover Design: Prajakta Sawant

STORYMIRROR
Stories that reflect you

Publisher: StoryMirror Infotech Pvt. Ltd.
Unit No-F/705, 7th Floor Kailas Corporate Lounge,
Veer Savarkar Road, Vikhroli Park Site, Vikhroli West,
Mumbai-400079, Maharashtra, India.

Web: storymirror.com
Facebook: @storymirror
Instagram: @storymirror
Twitter: @story_mirror
Contact Us: marketing@storymirror.com

To people everywhere
often derogatorily referred to
as 'consumers'

# ACKNOWLEDGEMENTS

Heartfelt thanks to Bibhu, Riddhi, Sneha, Harshitha, Shreya, Esha, and everyone at StoryMirror for making this book possible.

I am grateful to my dear friends and colleagues who took the time to review the manuscript and provide their valuable comments: Viresh for his logical arguments and detailed thoughts; Bhalekar for adding a touch of positivity; Saba for his marketing savvy and compelling business storytelling that rubbed off on me, eventually; and Prakash for sharing his practical wisdom.

Also, thanks to all those who have provided their encouragement and support: Sayed Sarwar Ali who has been a family friend, mentor, and guide; and the IIT-B batch of 1990 especially Anu, Sanjay, TK, Wanage, Wilfred, Alluri, Surya, Shashi, Senthil, and the rest of the gang. Thanks to Suhas, Seebah, VD, and Santosa for sharing their amazing stories, and Bhatta for setting me off on this journey all those years ago.

What I owe my family really can't be put into words. I'm deeply grateful to my parents for, above all, introducing me to the world of books; my sister for her unconditional support; and my wife and son for making me believe, and putting up with my numerous foibles.

# INTRODUCTION

"And a lovely revolution to you too, sir."

On 25 January 2011, a young economics consultant in Cairo, known only as TravellerW, pulled out his mobile phone at 11.42 am and tweeted out those words.

Tension had been brewing for days in Egypt, with vast sections of the population fed up with the country's leadership.

Some minutes later there was a reply, "Internet's back in #Egypt." Shortly after came another reply, and another, and another.

A couple of hours later the tweets began to get ominous, "This will get ugly quick," Sandmonkey tweeted.

And get ugly it did.

Security forces disguised as civilians were joined by thugs and penetrated the pro-change demonstrators who had taken to the streets. They led a charge on horses and camels, whipping the crowds as they rode through.

Rocks were thrown at them. They retaliated with guns and tanks.

The pro-change demonstrators suffered terrible losses. But they refused to budge. By the next day, they had pushed back the tyrannical security forces and taken over the city.

Soon the dictatorship fell.

It all started with those few words, typed into a mobile screen, which snowballed into a deluge of tweets as thousands of people poured into the streets, capturing the imagination of millions around the world—no mean feat in this age of allegedly declining attention spans—and started a revolution that resulted in the toppling of the ruling government in Egypt.

It has often been showcased as the ultimate testimony to the power of digital communications.

Soon afterwards, in a different part of the world, a girl named Malala Yousafzai, all of 13 years old at the time, had a burning wish for something many of us take for granted—she wanted to go to school.

Just for having this desire, Malala was shot in the head. It was an assassination attempt by the Taliban while she was in a school bus in the Swat district of northwestern Pakistan.

They failed. She survived.

A year later, in 2013, armed with a smart phone and zero marketing budget, she achieved the reach and power that media corporations would have given an arm and a leg for, a few decades ago.

While digital communications have made reaching out to millions of the proverbial target audience cheaper and easier than ever before, world-changing messages like those by TravellerW and Malala are, by far, the exception.

The paradox is that though there are literally hundreds and thousands of communication channels today to connect with, well, whoever you want, making a real connection with one's intended—and sometimes unsuspecting—audience has become even more elusive, not easier than before.

An old concept that is getting renewed attention today is the hierarchy of human needs by Abraham Maslow. It is encapsulated in a pyramid with the lower levels describing basic physiological needs and progressing step-by-step to the ultimate goal of human existence—self actualization.

*Fig. 1: Maslow's Hierarchy of Needs*

In his wonderful book, Winning the Story Wars[1] author Jonah Sachs espouses the idea of empowerment marketing. He contends that almost all of the marketing we see today is based on Freudian thought, wildly popularized by his nephew Edward L. Bernays, which is in direct opposition to Maslow's ideas.

While Freud believed that all of humanity spends their entire life in lowest section of the pyramid—dealing with sex and greed—Maslow held out a little more hope for us, believing that we are basically designed for self actualization, the highest section of the pyramid, pursuing wholeness, perfection, justice, richness, simplicity, beauty, truth, uniqueness, and joy.

If all our marketing from the last century or so till today had been based on Maslow's ideas, the world would probably have been a much different—and much better—place than it is today.

Instead, we were led down the Freudian path, and almost all of our marketing until recently is based on appeals to the basest of human instincts: greed, sex, money, and power.

Freudian ideas permeated almost every single message ever broadcast over the last century.

How to be more sexy.

How to show off your status.

How to beat your competition.

As a consequence, we as individuals and as a species have fallen far short of the ideal of achievement and human potential that was—and still is—open to us.

Maslow's ideas are creeping into communications today, but Freudian concepts are so deeply ingrained in the marketers' psyches that even when some do take the 'empowerment' route, as many have begun to recently, the noble and inspiring ideas expressed by some of these marketing messages have little real connection with the actual products. The results are, sadly, shallow at best and deceptive at worst.

To get to a better place, communications in general, and marketing as a field in particular, really need to be reinvented and their scope broadened to accommodate a more holistic view of why we are here on this planet. Our existence is much, much more than a series of decisions about what to buy—at least it ought to be.

We deal with altogether too much stuff in our lives. Time has shown us over and over again that much of the stuff we have used is either detrimental to our health and well-being or society or the environment.

Many wildly successful campaigns have been created around this theme, such as The Story of Stuff series by Annie Leonard and Jonah Sachs.

Obviously, not all products are evil. There are great products today, that have stood the test of time or embody the lessons learnt from past mistakes. They represent the best of human innovation and effort. Their souls need to be explored and their stories need to be told.

Hopefully this book will help you to tell the story better.

# CONTENTS

# 1

# SO WHAT'S DIFFERENT ABOUT THE DIGITAL ERA?

The digital age has transformed the way we live and communicate in at least three major ways:

## 1. THE POWER SHIFT

There was a time, not so long ago, when advertisers and marketers could, without a second thought, book a prime time slot on major TV channels, a solus position advertisement slot in mainstream newspapers, and possibly throw in a few larger-than-life outdoor spots, and be done with it.

Media planning was a perfect science.

Communication was a one-way street.

The company could say whatever it wanted and all that the customer could do—was expected to do—was shut up and listen.

A company that cared would add a toll-free customer helpline—usually in small print. The only 'power' the customer had was to call that helpline, or approach a local newspaper or consumer court in case of more serious problems with the company or its products or services, and pray that they would be heard.

In the digital era, especially with the rise and rise of social media, the power now lies firmly in the hands of the consumer. The boot is now firmly on the other foot—and, gosh, it pinches!

Companies today have shifted—been forced to shift—from the old 'me big gorilla' positioning to something on the lines of 'me and you together'.

It's a good start for sure, but probably not quite enough.

## 2. DEATH BY CHOICE

We are laden with choices, choices, and then some.

From a brand communicator's perspective, where it was just a question of deciding what to say, it's now a question of first deciding where to say it, choosing from the plethora of channels—social or print or TV or events or mobiles or wearables or Out Of Home or Digital Out Of Home—and then deciding what to say. With the widely differing formats and tastes peculiar to each medium, very often it means saying *entirely different things* on different channels.

Since its birth in the late 1990s, digital communications has proliferated and metamorphosed into a larger-than-life entity with its own unique language and jargon.

It began unassumingly enough with words like eyeballs, keywords, and search engines.

Soon, however, it spun out of control to make way for downright scary terms like ATF, site authority, bounce rates, CTA, CTR, CPC, CAC, PPC, PPA, LTV, SMM, SERP, Panda algorithms—and even Google Dances!

The list grows longer every day.

In stark contrast, the digital era has given marketing's sibling—advertising—some sort of an identity crisis.

Advertising has died several deaths since the dawn of the Internet and been unceremoniously buried each time, yet just like demons in horror movies, it seems to come back to life again and again.

From a citizen's perspective, the plethora of choices has resulted in a 360° deluge of content. What has certainly increased is the quantity of choices. Quality however remains a different question altogether.

It also means that people are now liable to change brand loyalties relatively easily. Mere decades ago, brand loyalty was for keeps. It was not unusual for people to stay true to their favorite brands for a lifetime, even across generations. Those days are gone with the wind of change brought by digital communications.

## 3. HELLO WORLD

Today brands—as individuals or organizations—no longer talk only to a particular group but rather to diverse, geographically dispersed groups, with very divergent values.

For those hapless copywriters tasked with creating global communications, this has compounded the problem of creating engaging copy. No more can they rely merely on an eloquent turn of phrase to build a brand.

Now, cultural sensitivity is as much a necessary part of a communicator's arsenal as clever words. The inescapable need to translate campaigns into different languages calls for 'language-independent' ideas.

Basically this means that communications now have to be more simple and direct.

Come to think of it, communication should have become easier, actually.

So why hasn't it?

# 2

# HOW DIGITAL COMMUNICATIONS CAN TRANSFORM INDIVIDUALS, BUSINESSES, AND SOCIETY

The English computer scientist, Timothy John Berners-Lee, the inventor of the Internet said, "The Web as I envisaged it, we have not seen it yet. The future is still so much bigger than the past."

To date, billions of ordinary people have come up with ordinary ideas but occasionally there is a glimmer of hope. Sometimes ordinary people reach out and do extraordinary things. A TravellerW rouses a nation and a Malala rallies the entire world around an idea of empowerment and transformation—and that is what digital communications can be about.

It would be tragic to leave digital communications solely in the hands of marketers and the so-called 'influencers' of the marketplace.

The medium is too powerful to be utilized merely to sell products. It can, and ought to be a vehicle for the transformation of individuals, businesses, communities, and nations.

We create and disseminate messages every day, if not as a profession, then through our posts on social media sites and the instant messages we exchange with our friends and acquaintances, and the endless forwards, besides our conversations and emails and water cooler gossip.

In the digital era, *we are all communicators.*

In that sense, we have a responsibility to remember that each one of us is here on a journey to find fulfillment through self-expression, and every communicator is obliged to help viewers, readers, and listeners along the way.

Towards that aim, communicators need to abide by some fundamental rules. Some of them are about form, such as using appropriate media, minding one's language, and avoiding an over-emphasis on visuals. Many of them are about basic principles such as honesty, empowerment, and genuine empathy for people.

At first glance, these rules are simple to the point of being obvious but, as experience shows, incredibly hard to practice. It is, however, well worth the effort and discipline required to follow them.

# THE NO-NONSENSE DIGITAL MARKETING CHECKLIST

The questions on this checklist may seem blunt, even rude; however the point is hardly to offend readers or question their integrity. Slips can happen to the best of us. In a world overflowing with digital garbage—false hopes and unreal expectations, also called maya or illusions, the best one can do is not to inadvertently contribute to it.

# #1 DO YOU REALLY MEAN WHAT YOU POST?

You've probably heard variants of this story in school, involving wolves, but it's worth repeating.

In the town of Kajiado in Kenya, the lions from the nearby Nairobi National Park were frequent and unwelcome guests. The lions would then have to be hunted and captured, or killed, by the wildlife officials.

So when young Atieno ran into the town one afternoon screaming, "Lions! Lions!" it was natural for everyone to panic.

The wildlife officials were summoned.

The town's residents went on high alert, grabbing every stick and knife and sickle they could find.

After several hours of searching, however, no lions were found. The officials asked Atieno how many lions he had seen.

"Quite a few, sir."

The search continued. It was approaching dusk, and still no lions were found.

The officials asked the boy again, "How many lions, son?"

"Quite a few, from the sound of their roars, sir."

Again the weary officials returned to their search. It was dark, when they asked the boy, "Are you quite sure you saw these lions, boy?"

"Didn't really see them, sir, but I heard them loud and clear," Atieno replied nervously.

Now it was really late, and the officials were hungry and tired. Throwing caution to the winds, they spread out and a few hours later, were about to give up the search.

At the end of their patience, they snapped at Atieno, "Listen kid, were there or were there not any lions?"

"Well, actually I didn't hear them myself, but my friend, Ikeno, he heard them. Really loud and clear."

Needless to add, no lions were found that night.

***

One of the consequences of the digital era is that advertising and marketing communications have had to shift from selling products by creating grand designs and grander statements to designing consistent user experiences focused on solving problems.

To successfully communicate, whether as individuals or companies, political parties or organizations, marketing or spiritual gurus—anyone who wants to get a message across—we need to communicate in a believable way that addresses a pain of the listener, within a short time.

That is all that effective communication boils down to and those that are able to get this message across will succeed.

Those that don't will wither and perish.

It doesn't matter whether we spend nothing, a few dollars, a million, or even a billion.

It doesn't matter whether we use a single channel or all the media available to us.

The short time available to convey our message has nothing to do with people's diminishing attention spans. It has a lot to do with the deluge of garbage that passes off as communication. We are not competing with well-designed, utterly thought-provoking messaging. It's the opposite.

And if we're not careful, we're liable to end up with all the junk that floods people's lives.

There is a ray of hope, however, amidst this seemingly dismal state of affairs: *people do care.*

And if we're honest, smart, and relevant, our message *will* get all the attention it deserves.

That is, however, a double-edged sword, because it requires communicators to answer the often uncomfortable question: how *deserving of attention* is our message?

Many communicators aim to achieve something that is popularly called 'creating a buzz'—it could be around anything from product launches to political agendas, entertainment to enlightenment.

These are the Atienos of the communication world.

Whatever success this approach creates, unless it's backed by solid facts, is bound to fizzle out—and in the digital age, that is likely to happen sooner rather than later.

If this seems like stating the obvious, we need to look no further than our Spam folder and all the mails deleted from our Inboxes. If one ever has subscribed to a mailing list or newsletter or given out an email ID to a marketer, without putting our computer systems in complete state of lockdown, we know what the flood of garbage is like.

How many communicators actually mean what they say?

How many product claims, magical cures, exciting initiatives, and political propaganda do we actually believe?

As of 2017, more than 60% of all emails are spam. How many millions in wasted work hours and marketing spends does that add up to, which could have been put to better use elsewhere?

# #2 ARE YOU READY TO BE A GRAMMAR NAZI?

When Czar Nicholas Alexandrovich of Russia, also known as Alexander III, was crowned at the Kremlin in 1883, there were major conspiracies to eliminate him. Before he took over, his father, Alexander II had been killed in a bomb attack on his way to the palace.

One suspected conspirator had been caught and sentenced to life imprisonment in Siberia, which meant certain death.

The defendant made a plea for mercy.

It was turned down.

The Czar's warrant read, "Pardon impossible, to be sent to Siberia."

As the story goes, his wife Czarina Maria Fyodorovna chanced upon the document. For reasons unknown, she modified the document to read, "Pardon, impossible to be sent to Siberia."

Changing the position of the comma saved his life.

***

Communication in every language, in print and online, seems to be slowly sinking into a gray abyss of grammar hell. In English, these are some examples of cringe-worthy cluelessness we increasingly come across every day:

'Your' instead of 'you're' and *vice versa.*
'It's' instead of 'Its' and *vice versa.*
'There' instead of 'their' and *vice versa.*
'Slight of hand' instead of 'sleight of hand'.
'Avail' instead of 'avail of'.
'Role out' instead of 'roll out'.
'Should of' instead of 'should have'. Seriously.

The list is by no means exhaustive.

During the Gulf war in 1990-91, after over 100,000 sorties by the coalition in which 88,500 tons of bombs were dropped, a prominent U.S. general went on TV, saying that certain parts of Iraq had been 'rubblized'—a construction term for breaking down concrete using hydraulic breakers.

What he meant was that he had 'pulverized' the place—and the language with it.

Just as anyone pointing out the horrors of war is likely to be labeled as 'one of them', anyone calling out atrocious language is promptly labeled a Grammar Nazi, as if expecting basic spelling skills were a crime.

Perhaps, the growing focus on visual, and audio, and 'experiential' learning is turning us all into a bunch of knowledgeable illiterates.

At an indoor event, several larger-than-life sculptures of human figures, painstakingly created by the creative team, were peppered around the venue for publicity. The visitors to the event, who had flown in from around the world, loved the theme and the execution and were all praise for the event.

Just as the creative team began to bask in the warm glow of satisfaction that everything had gone off smoothly, their head of communications walked in and uttered the most dreaded words any professional ever hears, "There's a problem."

Their hearts skipped collective beats as their worst fears seemed to take shape.

Perhaps one of the sculptures had fallen on a guest?

"What happened?" one of the designers finally spluttered.

The head gestured conspiratorially to the team to follow him, and led them to a signboard outside the guests' room which said, 'Visitors Lounge'.

He looked at them, and they looked right back, puzzled.

Finally he spoke, leaning towards them, his voice dropping to a whisper, "The apostrophe is missing."

"What?" went the chorus as the whole team heaved collective sighs of relief, *"Is that all?"*

Though it is unlikely that the visitors would have missed the lounge and lost their way at the venue for the lack of an apostrophe, as the Czarina demonstrated, the position of a punctuation mark can spell life or death.

Some organizations, especially those that depend on communications, take this to extremes, and any deviation from that bible of English grammar, *The Elements of Style by Strunk & White,* is punishable by death—well, almost.

Unfortunately, such organizations are few and far between.

With the proliferation of short forms like 'lyk', words such as 'turnt', 'fleek', and 'bae', and sentences like 'u r d 1 4 me', and the simultaneous globalization of audiences, the future of intelligible communication looks decidedly dim.

Digital communications, specifically instant messaging, have been the main culprit in the spread of such short forms, fueled, no doubt, by the ever-popular illusion that we are all running out of time. The issues created by mental illusions are chaotic enough, without ill-constructed messages fired by a keypad-happy communicator adding to the confusion.

Such words and phrases can hardly be considered—one hopes—steps in the natural evolution of language, much less of humankind.

The best that communicators can do, irrespective of the language we use, is not be part of such atrocities.

Facepalm.

# #3 ARE YOU USING SQUARE PEGS FOR ROUND HOLES?

On the plains of the Kalahari, the manner in which hunters captured monkeys was simple and incredibly ingenious.

In the hollow trees dotting the landscape, they simply cut out a small hole, just large enough to let a monkey's open palm through, but not large enough for its clenched fist.

The hunters then left some peanuts inside the hollow trunk as bait.

It is amazing how many monkeys were captured just because they wouldn't open their fists and let go of the peanuts.

What is even more amazing is how many humans won't let go of outdated ideas, even at the cost of wasting billions of dollars.

***

The greatest example of this was banner advertising on the Internet. Website banners are the digital avatars of hoardings and posters in the brick-and-mortar world, and also perhaps the biggest and the most expensive flop in the history of advertising.

In the 1990s, the early days of the Internet, website banners were the rage, and still are, to a lesser extent, today. They owed their existence to the success of posters and hoardings in the 'real' world, because once we get hold of an idea, like the monkeys of the Kalahari, we find it hard to let go, even when its time has passed.

There is a humungous amount of data available on the movement of the eyes while reading. A simple observation of one's own eye movements, however, is sufficient to guess what the typical patterns are likely to be. The striking differences in print, online, and mobile patterns simply imply that what works in one medium almost certainly won't work in the others.

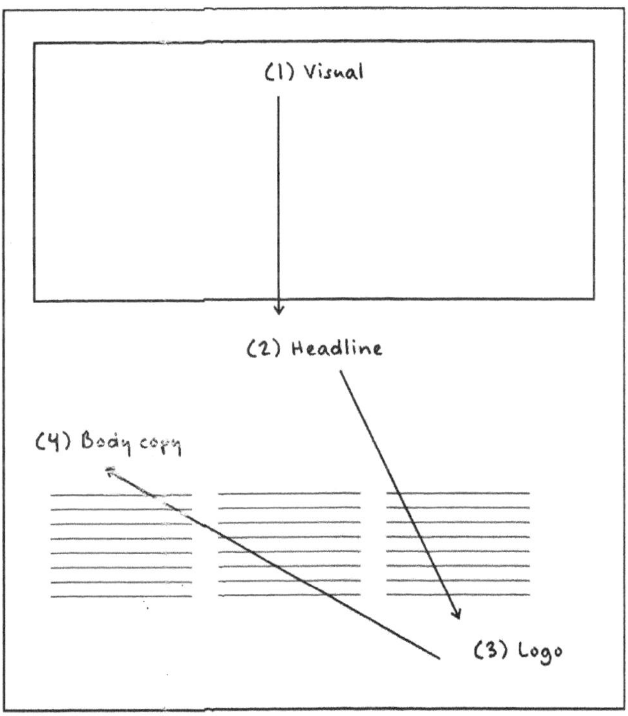


*Fig. 2: Eye movement when viewing a typical print advertisement*

The natural eye movement of the reader when viewing a print advertisement. It is textbook knowledge for anyone in the communications business that it is almost always the visual that catches the eye first, then the headline as the reader is 'drawn in' and tries to find out more about it.

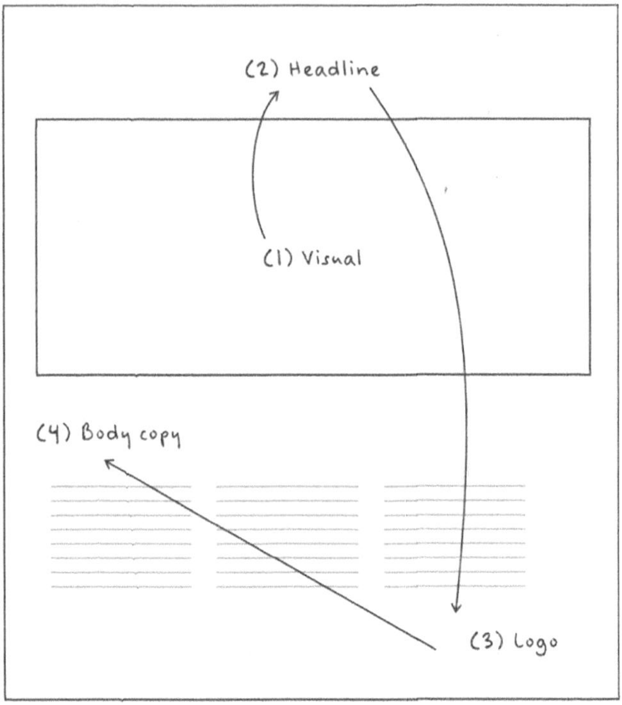


*Fig. 3: Eye movement when viewing another typical print advertisement*

Reversing the position of the headline and visual breaks up the natural eye movement, making it harder to read and consequently reducing impact and sales. Despite strong admonitions from such advertising legends as David Ogilvy, many art directors routinely commit this faux pas.

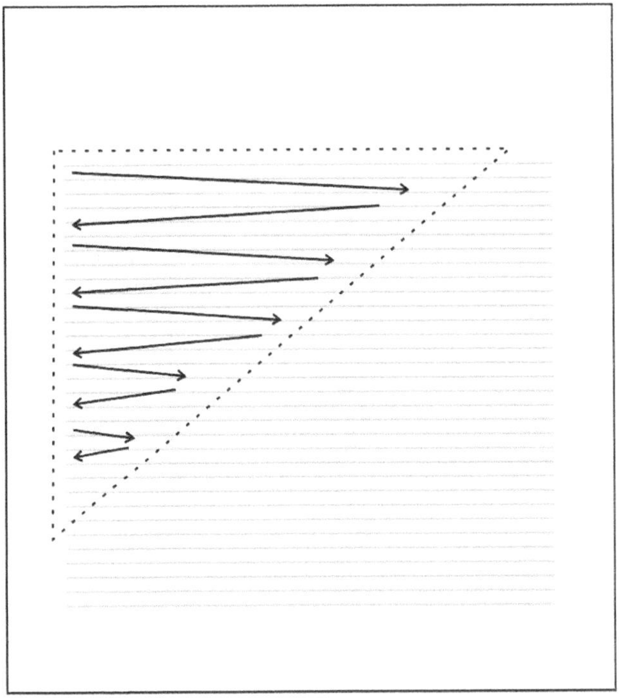

*Fig. 4: Eye movement when viewing a typical Web page*

The Web turned the conventional reading pattern on its head with the possibility of infinite vertical scrolling. The natural eye movement of the reader when viewing a Web page makes the chances of side-bar advertisements being noticed even lower than in print.

Some designers attempt to create a page-flip browsing experience by using a horizontal scroll, which apart from being counter-intuitive, is just plain painful.

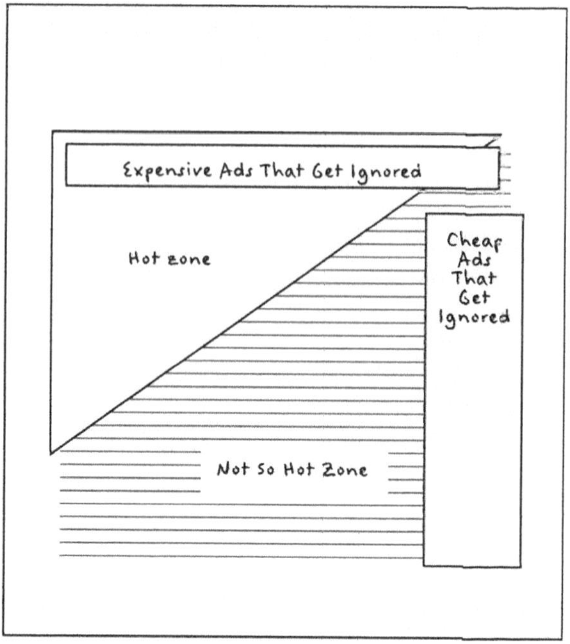


*Fig. 5: The so-called 'hot zone' in Web pages*

This is the triangular area, where most of the readers' time and attention is spent.

Who would know all this better than anyone else in the world?

Google.

The Google search results page is a fertile ground for any research on this topic. It's not surprising that the most expensive Google ads, the paid search results, are in the top of the triangle. The cheaper ads are in the zone that is more likely to be ignored.

Except for one thing: viewers now increasingly tend to ignore all ads.

Of course, Google knows this too.

So, over time the ads look less and less like ads, and more like the so-called 'organic' or genuine search results.

In a rather remarkable display of nimbleness for a mammoth, however, Google keeps changing its algorithms and the look of its search results.

By the time this book sees the light of day, all this may well have changed—yet again.

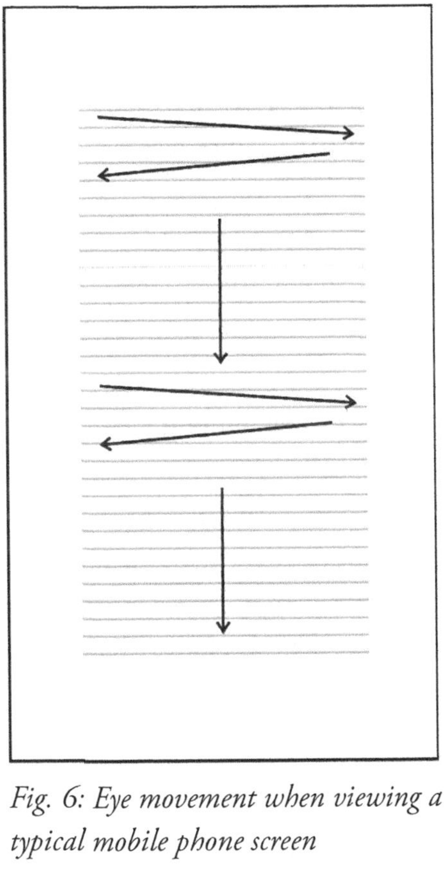

*Fig. 6: Eye movement when viewing a typical mobile phone screen*

Mobiles have opened another can of worms with the jerky, scroll-stop-scan eye movement of the reader when viewing a page. Naturally, mobile pages are even more of a hit-or-miss.

The very nature of mobile viewing necessitates vertical scrolling. So content that is 'below the fold'—not visible on the opening screen without scrolling down the page—actually has a better chance of being seen than its desktop counterpart.

There is not yet enough conclusive data on eye patterns for 'wearables' but we can count on it changing the ballgame yet again.

Communicators need to learn from those banner ads—that were basically 'digital posters', and never really worked well enough to ever justify their price tags.

The same goes for TV commercials that are repeated on online video channels. While TV is one-way, the Internet is a two-way street. Plugging intrusive commercials before videos actively encourages viewers to hate the brand, and eagerly search for the 'skip' button.

To have viewers react, "Get out of my face!" is worse than not publishing a video at all.

A much better option is to leverage the two-way nature of the medium, and engage viewers with an interactive, mutually beneficial experience. Simply replaying TV spots online is lazy thinking—never the best strategy for success.

Methods that work for the 'old' media, such as print, TV and outdoor, need not necessarily work in digital communications.

In fact, they almost certainly will not.

Swipe your smart watch screen, anyone?

# #4 ARE YOU ADDING TO THE DIGITAL GARBAGE PILE?

When Roger lost his father, it was all the more tragic because his death was unnecessary—collateral damage in an insane war between megalomaniacs and politicians.

Most children would be crushed by a tragedy like that.

Not this lad.

He sublimated his anguish, transforming his sadness into one of the most successful musical productions in history.

In 1979 Roger Waters' concept album, The Wall went platinum twenty-three times over and sold over 19 million copies worldwide.

Phrases from the album, such as "We don't need no education," became a mantra for generations to come.

His angst is palpable when he spits out lyrics such as, "Got thirteen channels of sh*t on the TV to choose from."

So, who built the wall? And, how do we tear it down?

Since the album was released in 1979, things are decidedly worse in many ways.

The needless wars and death tolls keep rising.

The 'regular' educational system not only enslaves rather than frees the mind, it is now getting unaffordable for many.

In the context of communications, the thirteen TV channels are now north of thirteen thousand at a conservative estimate.

***

The two-percent rule in marketing basically states that only 2% of any marketing messages get any attention. The remaining 98% are treated as junk and summarily ignored.

This is best known to the direct marketing tribe, where the rule-of-thumb is that if you send out a hundred mailers, only two people are likely to respond.

While digital marketing has made it easier to reach people, the flip side is that it also makes it easier for people to avoid you. The traditional cold calls and printed direct mailers are relatively harder to get rid of. People do answer calls, even if it is just to say a brusque, "Not interested." The contents of envelopes do get a peek, even if they're on the way to wastepaper baskets.

Deleting an unwanted email, on the other hand, is ridiculously easy.

Click. And poof. You're gone forever.

Things have gotten progressively worse since The Wall and, with the tsunami of mobile apps and what-nots, are way out of control.

This investor-fueled mania continues despite the fact that 65% of smart phone users *do not download any apps at all.*(2)

The result of all the never-ending stream of digital clutter is that essentially even hoping for a 2% success rate is a bit of a luxury. Probably the old marketing thumb rule needs to be updated and renamed as the 0.2% rule.

Again, it's not marvelous and brilliant messages by competitors that are the problem—it's the 99.8% of digital garbage.

Those of us who aren't careful will end up getting flushed.

# #5 ARE YOU PRIORITIZING BIG IDEAS OVER BIG VALUE?

When a micro-sized greeting card manufacturing company with an even more micro-sized budget needed copywriters and art directors, this is what their ad agency came up with.

*Fig. 7: A really tiny advertisement*

It was the tiniest-sized advertisement, created in the days before email and the Internet. It produced so many responses, the client ran out of fax paper rolls.

Sometimes it doesn't take a great headline and stunning visual—the strongest message can merely be a statement of fact. And it doesn't require the product on sale to be a Rolls Royce either.[3]

***

The so-called 'big idea' has been bandied about so much and for so long, it has taken on a life of its own, becoming a cliché in communication circles.

If you've ever written or planned to write an advertisement, or article, or even an invitation to your kid's birthday party, you've probably encountered the question: what's the big idea?

And if one is in the communications business, the more important query would be: how do we get to the big idea?

Does it come from our mind?

Does it arise out of an in-depth understanding of our product or subject?

Does it flow out of a bottle of alcohol, as many famous copywriters say?

Does it stem from the perceptions in people's minds, as marketing gurus claim?

YMMV. Your mileage may vary.

Generally 'big ideas' are construed to be something outrageous, something earth-shattering, something that has never been 'done' before. This approach, unfortunately, firmly puts the cart before the horse.

The real answer to 'what's the big idea?' is a counter question: what's the big value we are offering the reader?

# #6 WILL YOUR MARKETING EMPOWER PEOPLE, LIKE REALLY?

In July 1998, at a university office in the UK, the phone rang. The caller claimed he wanted to donate 'some money' to them to fund a professorship. Considering it to be a prank, the university staff rudely dismissed him and disconnected the call.

A while later, the University of Glasgow received a similar call. They were far warmer in their response.

A while later, they received a check from an individual in Las Vegas—for £1.2 million.

They founded a chair in the donor's name: the William R Lindsay Chair in Health Policy and Economic Evaluation.[4]

***

Stop press. Empowerment, still in its infancy as a communications concept, has already been hijacked. And it is being used to market, among other undesirables, probably the least empowering product ever created—alcohol.

Imagine the magnitude of irony when an alcohol manufacturer blithely talks about doing good, making the world better, winning the right way, or depicts some other genuine achievement.

Do something memorable. *Drink alcohol.*
Be a marketing genius. *Drink alcohol.*
Save a drought-stricken village. *Drink alcohol.*
And then there's the ubiquitous *drink responsibly.*

What next? Burglars putting up posters advising citizens to 'secure your homes' perhaps?

If the hero or heroine of the slickly produced TV spots actually consumed alcohol regularly, it is unlikely he or she would have achieved much more than a daily hangover. To create an association between alcohol and achievement is about as credible as a fascist making speeches on world peace.

The objective of such 'empowerment' is just to assuage the feelings of guilt every person who consumes alcohol feels, especially the morning after a binge. It seeks to pacify the drinker that, hey, look, here's someone who achieved something worthwhile—and she or he drinks.

Except for one thing: that person doesn't exist.

If ever there was any achievement made by an alcoholic, it would be despite the booze, certainly not because of it.

The foundation of empowerment is honesty. One definition of honesty is to keep thoughts, words, and actions in sync. So when alcohol companies talk about 'doing good' for the world, something is definitely way out of place.

Alcohol manufacturers are by no means the only industry to eagerly hop onto the empowerment bandwagon. We find an ever-increasing number of such self-proclaimed do-gooders wearing the unlikeliest of garbs.

The banking and insurance sector, for example, whose business model for the most part, in the most rudimentary terms, is to charge people for using their own money.

The telecom sector is another, about which the less is spoken the better.

And so it goes.

It's not all bleak and gray a picture. There are individuals and companies that have transformed entire villages and towns, genuinely improved education and living conditions, and empowered citizens.

If a girl who had never been educated can go to a school in her neighborhood, it is empowerment.

If poor villagers in a developing country find the means to finance their livelihood without getting killed by interest rates, use hygienic toilets where there were none, access clean drinking water without having to walk for miles in a desert, all that is empowerment.

Our focus as organizations, or as individuals as in the case of William Lindsay, has to be on *genuine* empowerment—to walk the talk.

So, what's the solution to alcohol manufacturers talking about empowerment?

It is too easy to take measures like banning alcohol or penalizing companies, but they simply don't work. Prohibition, for instance, will probably go down in history as the greatest failed experiment of all time. It is an open secret that states that enforced prohibition pegged—no pun intended—alcohol consumption levels that are at par with, and sometimes higher than, other states where booze flows freely.

That's simply how our minds work. If someone tells us not to think of elephants, what is the first thought that comes to mind?

To use force is to suppress. Force reinforces illusions because it works on the same level of consciousness where the problem exists. To escape the web of *maya* requires the conscious cultivation of its opposite—awareness.

Building awareness requires making real connections through honest communication, not noble-sounding words.

We, as individuals or business entities, can only grow and prosper *in collaboration with* the people we communicate with. There are limits to the extent we can profit from their ignorance and those limits will be breached sooner rather than later.

# #7 ARE YOU KEEPING IT REAL?

Not so long ago, a diesel engine manufacturer had a problem. Their product was technologically at par, if not better, than others. It was doing okay but new competitors were cropping up.

The senior management wanted change. Now, change in itself is not a bad thing, of course; it is inevitable.

However the change that this company wanted was to enable people to 'relate to'—a euphemism for 'buy'—their products.

They hired one of the world's biggest advertising agencies and tasked them with this ambitious vision. A few months and several million dollars later, the agency had pulled the message of 'spreading happiness' out of the magic hat that all agencies have.

Happiness is what we all seek, the focus groups revealed, and if the company could claim that it spread happiness, the market was theirs.

The senior management loved it and the 'happiness engine' was born.

You may or may not have met buyers and users of diesel engines, but what do you think their primary concerns are likely to be?

Perhaps, how noisy the darn things are?

How much fuel they guzzled?

How they pollute the environment?

Can you conceive of a person who would relate a diesel engine with happiness? If anyone wanted happiness, presumably they would turn to their families or get a hobby or pursue some personal achievement; certainly not switch on their diesel engines.

Nevertheless, the campaign was launched. Every mainstream newspaper, every billboard on every highway screamed about the 'happiness engine'.

It was a disaster of mythological proportions, but nobody except the senior management was surprised. The agency skipped off to find their next victim—quite happily.

We find plenty of such examples of misguided attempts at 'connecting with consumers'.

***

Professional communicators have subverted so many words of the language that readers are immune to their presence. Using these 'invisible' words is simply a waste of space, and usually, money as well.

Words that are best avoided are: future, innovation, imagination, performance, success, challenges, together, value, care, connected, passion, commitment, leadership, excellence, service, possibility, life, trust, designed, and (the word) more. These are all fine values, and the problem is that every business has them in some form or the other. At least they should.

What we need to do is keep communication simple.

Keep it honest.

Keep it real.

People appreciate it when we are upfront about what we want. If we are selling something, we really ought not to pretend we are there for something else.

Another thing people and organizations really don't need to do is pursue the most illusory of goals—a 'desirable brand image'.

An organization's brand image starts and ends with the human beings who use its products and services. In the case of individuals it is our persona among friends and colleagues. If relating with them is the goal, as was the case with the diesel engine manufacturer, then by all means we should relate—with actual people.

It is a fatal error to try to superimpose our creative vision—or the CEO's vision—of how the world is, and try to 'create an image' of how reality ought to be.

Reality exists as it is, with or without us, thank you very much.

The disconnection with reality is the cause of the silent, unpublicized failure of an unflattering number of communication campaigns worldwide.

A common cause for this disconnection is the desire to make products appear cool, which in turn stems from the illusion that being cool is a worthy goal, or even a goal at all.

Reality is often less than cool. Sometimes it is very un-cool.

We need to deal with reality, as early as possible, or our communications will be no more than empty—and rather expensive—shots fired into the wind.

# #8 WHAT DOES YOUR LOGO SAY ABOUT YOU?

On 16 September 2008, the world witnessed an unimaginable disaster when the bottom fell out of the financial markets.

Within days, entire countries went bankrupt.

Stock exchanges were shut down to stop the mad rush to the exit.

Amidst all the chaos, an unlikely investor doubled his investment. When asked how he managed it, he claimed there were only three things he looked at when buying stocks.

The first was, of course, the price of a company's shares, in relation to its earning potential, viz., the P/E ratio. Next he considered the amount of loans the company had taken, its debt.

It's quite normal for any investor to scrutinize both these factors. It was the third that was unusual.

For the third parameter he looked at was the company logo.

Our logos can tell others a lot more than we may imagine—sometimes more than we may want.

***

If you come across a logo with a coat of arms, chances are you are dealing with a royal family, or an alcohol manufacturer, or a tobacco company. Two out of these, perhaps all three, can be dangerous for health.

Overly intricate designs seem to suggest there is an elaborately fabricated tale being told—otherwise known as a 'con job'. Companies with such logos need to change them or rapidly fade into irrelevance.

How do we know a logo is 'right'?

While there are plenty of design standards that can fill an entire undergraduate program, it boils down to good taste. Those who are serious about communication need to invest in a good designer. Logos are the face of the company for life, sometimes spanning generations.

If there is one blunder a company can make, it is to allow the CEO to micromanage design—unless he's Steve Jobs. (Incidentally, he ascribed a lot of Apple's 'design success' to good typography.)

For instance, there was a CEO of a company who insisted their logo should have *a tree, multiple branches, and different varieties of fruits.* He went to specify that there should be an apple, an orange, a pineapple, a banana, and perhaps some more, that he generously left to the creativity of the design team.

They were into the business of logistics. Nothing to do with fruits nor trees. They delivered *envelopes.*

Their agency quit in frustration.

There is the other extreme, where the company takes its logo design, or re-design, way too seriously.

For instance, Pepsi has changed its logo more than two dozen times.†

In recent times, there have been major global companies who widely publicized their logo redesigns, which seemed to have achieved little more than making their agencies some easy money.

So long as a logo is 'good', there really is no need to change it. As the saying goes, you don't need to fix what is not broken.

What is broken is our world and our society. Fixing them would be much more appreciated.

Many companies feel that having an old-fashioned logo makes them look like dinosaurs. They feel that logos need to change with the times.

Maybe.

Or maybe not—an old fashioned logo suggests that it's a company with a heritage, which is an attribute no brand can purchase.

For a newly formed company, the logo is the first and strongest opportunity to create a powerful brand. For the others, there's not much one can do, especially in an established company. Efforts to change logos are as likely to confuse customers as

† A fact well exploited by Coke in one of its advertisements.

they are to enlighten them. As such they are best left alone, unless there are serious issues or events, such as a merger or joint venture on the anvil.

So, how do we know if our logo is good enough?

The elements of a good logo are that it answers these three questions:

1. *Is it us?* Does it convey what we do or stand for? E.g., the A-Z in the Amazon logo.

2. *Is it smart?* E.g., the arrow in the FedEx logo.

3. *Is it simple?* E.g., the Google logo, whose playful variations defy all branding conventions.

With logos, we can apply the same thumb rule that works for jokes: if it needs explaining, it's not working.

# #9 DO YOU OVER-THINK VISUALS?

When Santosa graduated from art school and signed up to join one of the biggest global advertising agencies, he wasn't quite prepared for the real world.

The art directors there took their obsession with visuals to surreal extremes, however, and would demand the craziest things.

There was an advertisement he worked on that was set against a black background. Looking at his artwork, the art director raised a critical eyebrow and said, "This black is too black."

This was before '50 shades' became a part of the lexicon, so the poor chap couldn't even make a wisecrack about it.

On another occasion, when he was working on a website design, the reviewer looked at the screen from all angles and finally commented, "Move the image by half a pixel."

Apart from the fact that black is black, and that for most practical purposes it is physically impossible to move anything by half a pixel, which is the smallest unit of a display screen, such meaningless endeavors do little to add value to communications, and only serve to reinforce the hatred for such art directors in design circles.

***

Next in importance after the logo is the 'look-and-feel' of our communication.

What every art director worth her digital pen knows is that visuals need to telegraph the message.

In static images, it is the chewed up pencil that depicts stress.

In movies, it is the half-smoked cigar stubs that tell a predator how close he is to his prey (remember the sequence where Tuco tracks Blondie in the epic Hollywood western, *The Good, the Bad, and the Ugly?*)

Rumor has it that, once upon a time, the legendary PG Wodehouse was traveling by boat, when one of his co-passengers discovered who he was, and arranged an impromptu story-reading session.

Apparently, Wodehouse's narration lacked the energy of his prose, and the audience slowly dissolved till barely a soul was left.

To his credit, the great man stoutly droned on through the night till the wee hours of morning, even with no one to hear him.

Even a *great* story can be killed by the way it is told.

# #10 IS WINNING AWARDS YOUR GOAL?

There was a famous surgeon, who was called upon to operate on a patient in critical condition.

The surgeon, drawing upon his vast and formidable expertise, decided upon a surgery that had never been performed before in the world.

After many hours of labor, he stepped out of the operating theater and proudly announced, "The operation was successful... but the patient died."

Likewise, many advertising agencies have won major awards, while their clients went out of business.

***

When our communication talks about how great our products are, it is merely poor form—we really should talk about how those products serve people.

When our communication talks about how great our advertising agency is, it can be fatal.

One of the victims of its own creativity was Iridium, the satellite phone company. Its 'geography is history' campaign was simply brilliant, and flooded media channels worldwide, reportedly at a cost of $60 million at 1998 prices.

It is one of the primary requirements before any product launch to check the audience's reaction to, among other things, the price. Whether it was the client or the agency that miscalculated or failed is moot.

The product is history.

The litmus test for any campaign is the reaction of the audience.

If people go, "What a brilliant idea," we can safely assume that we're in trouble.

On the other hand, if they say, "What a brilliant product," we have a future.

There's nothing wrong, of course, with winning an award, but organizations that sense that their communications agency is *gunning* for an award need to fire them. Immediately.

# #11 ARE YOU PREPARED TO BE UNSOCIAL?

Predators in any jungle need to cover large areas to find prey. For instance, African lions have a 'home turf' of about 100 square miles.

Physically traversing every inch of this vast expanse is an impossible task, and in the struggle to survive, many of these hunters have found a simple solution.

It is based on the fact that, while the land areas are huge, the water bodies are far fewer in number and smaller in size.

And, no matter what the risk, one of the things that the prey cannot do without is visiting those ponds.

So, rather than sweat it out on foot, predators simply laze around near waterholes, knowing that, sooner or later, the prey *will* arrive.

And when they do, that's when they go for the kill.

Contextual advertising is a lot like that.

What is quite a fine strategy for animals is not so good for human beings. Yet many marketers brazenly hang out where their 'prey' are sure to land up, sooner or later—social media sites.

Except that people don't like to be preyed on. Of course, neither do animals, for that matter.

***

Being an 'unsocial' organization, or individual, does not mean what it sounds like.

By all means, create your Facebook business page, official Twitter handle, official YouTube channel, LinkedIn company profile, and everything else.

Just. Don't. Try. To. Sell.

The term 'social selling' is not just an oxymoron, it is obnoxious—at least to anyone who has been at the receiving end of it.

It's a lot like launching into a full-blown sales pitch to guests at a birthday party. Anyone who tries it will find themselves de-socialized fairly quickly.

In the late 1990s, we all witnessed the dotcom boom, followed by the bust from 2000–2002 in which many investors burned their fingers.

Looking at the social media bubble today, it would seem that some lessons are hard to learn.

Today, every vacuum pump and welding rod manufacturer, every plumber and grocery store, basically every business owner with Internet access thinks about having 'social presence'.

This has quickly spawned opportunistic industries who sell Social Media Marketing services. That bête noir of marketing,

Search Engine Optimization, a.k.a. SEO, has now been replaced by Social Media Optimization.

In the first place, asking an external agency to 'manage' our social media is like asking a stranger to take one's spouse out to dinner.

Secondly, just as email is great for sending letters, not unsolicited offers from content marketing cartels, social media are super for sharing stuff.

*Sharing*—not selling.

Communicators seem to have an incredibly hard time wrapping their brains around this.

People who visit social sites to 'consume' content do so for one of only three reasons:

1. Catch up with friends
2. Be entertained
3. Improve knowledge/income/career

So when a company shows up at a social site, they are as out of place as a vacuum cleaner salesman at a wedding.

A foray into social media usually heralds a moment-of-truth for companies—do they actually have *anything of value* to share?

Is their claim of 'enriching lives' for real or just another boilerplate slogan?

Having said that, there are areas where companies can make a real and valuable difference using social media, viz., disaster management and public service—in other words, *helping other people, which is what being sociable is about.* Surprise!

Social media also offer great opportunities for communicators, now better known as 'content developers'—both individuals and businesses—to deliver value, whether it is by thought leadership articles, videos, presentations, community conversations, and much more.

By its very nature, the medium is dynamic and in constant flux, so it is a good idea to be prepared for a long haul.

Have a content calendar.

Create a media plan.

Just don't count on peddling wares.

*People do not go to social sites to buy stuff.*

Buyers go to Amazon or Ebay or a million other sites that are honest about their business. Nobody apart from the company's marketing team and their agency really gives two hoots about that super creative advert or marketing message.

Pictures of welding rods and vacuum pumps just don't look right next to pictures of their kids playing with their cats.

Yet marketers don't just keep churning out content, they try to achieve 'scale'—which usually means about 100,000 social connections. The point-two-percent rule, however, means that for every 200 positive connections, we run the possible risk of making 99,800 people hate us.

Is it worth it?

While contextual advertisements have come a long way from the infamous advertisement for suitcases that appeared next to the horrifying news about a serial killer who disposed of bodies in suitcases, they haven't ceased to irritate.

We simply cannot make people buy by hitting them regularly on the head with our product.

In fact, anywhere between half and four-fifths of the younger generation—the much-sought-after 'category' of millennials—hate social media advertising so much that they actually disconnect themselves from the offending networks.

Perhaps even the term 'social' is a misnomer. According to several surveys, feeling dissatisfied and depressed is common after visiting social sites, especially after viewing others' vacation photographs. The impact of social networking sites on divorces is rising too.

While the humongous amount of data stored and generated by social networks—the so-called 'Big Data'—all of their data adds up to less than a tiny fraction of the data stored in human DNA.

For instance, all the data from Google, Facebook, and major tech companies can be stored in 1 gram of human DNA, which can hold 455 exabytes—an exabyte is one billion GB—of data.[5]

In other words, human potential is *several thousand orders of magnitude higher* than the level even the biggest networks operate on, and presents the biggest real opportunity that social media offer, which is largely overlooked in the mad scramble for 'likes', 'shares', 're-tweets', and what-nots.

This goldmine of human potential can only by tapped into with a collaborative, not a competitive, mindset.

To understand this opportunity, we need to head back once more to Maslow's pyramid, which defines the ultimate human purpose as the progressive quest for safety, love, belonging, esteem, and self-actualization.

The question that creators of social media content need to ask is: how can our ideas, our businesses, or our products *take on greater meaning?*

Something more worthy of our precious life than buying a bigger toy than our neighbor's.

Some goal nobler than getting richer than our fellow beings.

If we can genuinely answer this question—and resist scratching the itch to sell—social media offer one of the greatest opportunities in the history of humanity to forge enduring connections with people, while building our businesses.

It calls for an almost Zen-like ability of clapping with one hand, or fighting without fighting, or something like that.

What makes this more than mere intellectualization is the fact that some companies and individuals—very few, you can count them on your fingers—have achieved it.

They do it by going beyond simply mouthing some noble goals to actually living them out.

# #12 CAN YOU STICK TO THE BEST POLICY?

India is a country where, over the course of its history spanning several thousands of years, people evolved several simple, natural, inexpensive, home-grown solutions for many things—one of them is dental care.

These traditional solutions included using chewing twigs of *neem* or Indian Lilac, and 'brushing' with salt and charcoal.

In the 1970s, a leading toothpaste manufacturer took these traditions head-on, and challenged them with a blitz of advertisements that focused on the 'dangers' of such practices. Using toothpaste was modern and healthy, and those traditions were so un-cool.

If toothpastes really are the perfect answer for total dental care, why do we have so many dentists? That, however, isn't the point.

More recently, public opinion has swiveled back to traditional solutions, green ideas, and organic products.

Now, the very same toothpaste manufacturer has launched yet another advertising blitz about the 'dangers' of *not* using salt and charcoal.

Is it any wonder that nobody believes marketing communication?

***

It's the very creators of such ill-informed, half-baked messaging who have painted themselves into a corner. And that is a real tragedy, because the communications industry worldwide employs some of the finest minds, which come up with the most ingenious ideas and the wittiest observations, and could have been of far greater value and had more meaningful impact elsewhere, rather than in peddling toxic cosmetics and over-hyped products.

There is a ridiculously simple solution to the problem of being believable: *be honest.*

That's all there is to it.

Yet, marketers are way too smitten by Samuel Johnson's words, "Promise, large promise, is the soul of an advertisement."

This objective is often in direct opposition to the facts.

Maybe the product is just boring.
The price is too high.
The look is just unimpressive.

Intrepid marketers work their way around this tiny inconvenience in various ways.

Some of this marketing *maya* is subtle, some of it is in your face, and you're probably familiar with them all.

# #13 DO YOU LEAN ON ASTERISKS AND OBELISKS?

There was an optician who had been in business for many decades, running a successful little store on a street corner.

When her son was old enough, she brought him to the store to teach him the art of selling.

"Know your customers and watch their reactions, son," she began. "When one walks into the store and asks about the price of our glasses, in a matter-of-fact voice, say it will be a hundred dollars.

"Pause for a second, and if there's no sign of any shock or surprise on their face, continue and say… for the frame. And fifty dollars for the lenses.

"Pause for a second again, and if there still is no sign of shock, say… each."

Many businesses adopt this pricing strategy.

***

How hard is it to state the actual price of a product *without any asterisks?*

About 90% of sales issues would simply go away if marketers stated prices upfront. The reason they don't is the fear that *so would 90% of their sales.*

What this actually boils down to then is a pricing problem—our supply and demand curves don't intersect where we would like them to. Getting around this by creating an illusory 'sweet price' by using a ton of disclaimers and add-ons, however, eventually only ends up leaving a bitter taste in the mouth.

Asterisks can be the communication equivalent of *harakiri* in the long run.

Then we have statistics and slogans.

For instance, in a market for the same product category, how is it possible to have three different products that simultaneously claim to be 'the best', 'the leader', and 'number one'?

On closer inspection, we find that the product was 'the best' according to a certain survey conducted in a certain year.

Or that it is 'a leader' in a certain region.

Or that that it is 'number one' when ranked by a certain specific feature.

In a digital world, where comparative information is readily available to anyone who seeks it, such communication 'strategies' are more likely than not to end badly.

# #14 IS THERE ANY FINE PRINT?

With more than 1.25 billion people, India has one-fifth the world's population crammed into just 2.4% of the world's land area. Compared to the U.S., India has about four times the number of people with one-third the space.

One of the probable reasons for this is the importance that Indians place on marriage and children.

Mostly, we just don't stay single.

In fact, we practically *can't* stay single.

Whether you're a boy or girl, the moment you're of legal marriageable age, it becomes the concern of not just the parents but every uncle, aunt, neighbor, friend, and local grocer to find a bride/groom, who go, "Not married?" accompanied by a certain look, which basically means: *is there a problem?*

Until you finally succumb.
It doesn't end there.

The moment you're married, the same concerned folks are back, taking it to the next level. This time it's kids. Having kids is practically *compulsory*, to avoid more 'strange looks' from the rest of society—which is quite a large number of people.

The ubiquity of Indian marriages has less to do with exceptional romantic capabilities than with the common practice of 'arranged marriages', where the *parents or relatives* of the man and woman meet and decide that they can get married.

Usually the couple also do meet each other—briefly, if at all—before the wedding.

There have been instances when the man or woman who is 'presented' at this meeting turned out to be *a different person from the one who finally showed up on the wedding day,* hiding behind numerous flowery and ornamental veils.

While such practices are considered bizarre in India today, sometimes the marketing that is considered acceptable worldwide is no less so.

Often it is even more hazardous than marrying the wrong person.

***

We've all come across fine print that people with 20/20 vision would find hard to read.

This includes such whoppers as, "Side effects include blindness." Whoa.

*Caveat emptor*—it's the buyers job to beware.

There are terms like 'sugar free' which actually should be sugar replacement.

Then there are the multitude of terms bandied about, like insurance against fake brides and grooms. Here's just a minuscule sample.

Conditions apply.
Subject to market risks.
Cashless treatment.
Creative visualization.

Is that really what a person pays retail for—a 'creative visualization'?

Several companies around the world actively lobby against labeling genetically modified foods. Not content with getting away with ludicrous fine print, they would like to do away with it altogether.

In the U.S., for instance, this resulted in what has been dubbed the DARK (Deny Americans the Right to Know) Act, which makes GMO labeling an option, rather than a necessity.

If we go through the fine print of every product we consume, it's as likely to give us a heart attack as finding a stranger instead of our expected spouse-to-be at the wedding altar.

As a thumb rule, any text smaller than 10-point Helvetica is a definite red flag.

# #15 HAVE YOU EMBELLISHED FACTS?

At a presentation for an advertising campaign by a $100+ billion company, the communications agency showcased an idea that essentially claimed the company's product was 'the brand the world prefers'.

All statistics genuinely pointed to this being factually correct.

Yet, all the managing director had to say, in remarkable display of humility, and to the barely concealed amusement of the team, was, "Perhaps we should add 'we hope' to the headline."

Not all companies are congenitally dishonest, thankfully.

***

Some of us may have noticed that typically advertisements depict people who look like they just won the lottery.

Can a car, or detergent—or any product in the world—really make anyone *that happy?*

Beyond the fake happiness, there is a whole industry that survives on faking it.

In the cosmetics industry, all that this has achieved is to create mass, borderline depression amongst billions of women who never can hope to look as gorgeous as the models.

Beauty products are just the proverbial drop in the ocean.

Beyond the air brushing and photo-shopping, the fine art of photography is routinely prostituted to sell illusions.

For instance, marketing communications for dairy products use soap bubbles or glue to make milk and coffee look more tempting.

Engine oil instead of syrup.
Mashed potatoes instead of ice cream.
Shoe polish on grilled meat.
Glycerin on wine bottles.
Hairspray on fruits.

The concept of depicting products *as they are* is so alien to the communications industry that honesty in advertising is practically an oxymoron.

That is precisely what makes honesty such a precious commodity. *And that's what makes companies that practice it outstanding.*

As human beings, we generally try to hide vulnerability. After all, nobody likes to be perceived as weak.

What many communicators fail to see is that honesty is more valued than strength—especially fake strength.

If we could try being honest brands instead of 'strong' brands, we would be pleasantly surprised.

# #16 IS YOUR SOLUTION WORSE THAN THE PROBLEM?

You may have heard of the farmer who had a problem with rats. They hid in the hay in his barn, and wrecked his granary.

He was advised to buy a cat, which he did.

To feed the cat he needed milk.
So he bought a cow.
To feed the cow, he had to buy more hay.
And that just led to even more rats.

The basic problem with almost all marketing communication today is that it attempts to cajole us into, as the author Dave Ramsey said, "Buying things we don't need with money we don't have to impress people we don't like."

***

Retail therapy, the defining theme of our times, is in direct opposition to the great urges of humanity at large, to understand one's life purpose, find meaning, achieve a state of bliss, and to attain salvation. Serious and somber though these goals may seem, achieving them only has one requirement—*the ability to laugh.*

Do our products or our organizations genuinely increase the laughter in the world?

The kind of laughter, rooted in the pure unadulterated joy we experienced when were children—not the superficial jokes or slapstick humor that many companies indulge in.

Most product marketers do the opposite, spreading a feeling of discontent and creating a sense of scarcity, simply to achieve higher sales.

If you manufacture, say, nuts and bolts, it may be difficult to envision your products making people joyful, but it is *possible*. For instance, there is nothing more boring than the typical Monday morning office meeting. Yet, as Vitamins, a multidisciplinary design and invention studio based in London demonstrated, even something as mind-numbing as setting team schedules can be transformed into a joyful activity, which they did using Lego blocks.(6)

It is a question of reaching out and touching the inner child in everyone and there are millions of ways to do it, if we honestly search for them.

What does our inner child want?

To love and be loved.
To have good friends.

Never are fame, money, and achievements ever worthy goals in and of themselves. Relationships are the nuts and bolts of life itself. And it is possible for any company, including nut-and-bolt manufacturers, to infuse their products with genuine purpose.

# #17 ARE YOU DELIVERING VALUE FOR TIME?

Imagine that you want to buy a car and walk into a showroom, the car salesman shows you a fine vehicle, and goes into great detail about all the ways it meets your expectations.

You're impressed and decide to buy it.

And then the salesman mentions, almost in passing that, hey, by the way, the car only works for about 50% of the time, but you need to pay 100% of the price, and then glibly goes on to start talking about the various finance schemes and payment options you have.

Would you buy that car?

Of course not.

We are led on to believe that online media are different—umm, *how?*

***

The shortage of time that everyone supposedly faces today is no more clearly evident than in the billing criteria for social media advertisements: clients generally are made to pay for an advertisement—or what is now called an 'impression'—when at least 50% of the advertisement is visible on the user's computer or mobile phone screen for one second or more.

So, basically, companies pay when people see *half* of their advertisements for *one* second.

Seriously.

More than any tangible benefit to the clients who pay for this travesty, this just seems to be a desperate means to generate *some* revenue. We will doubtless find plenty of charts and graphs that proclaim the astounding benefits of social media marketing, or optimization, or whatever.

To estimate the degree of engagement any of these media generate, consider the verbs that are used to describe online activities:

- *Browsing* a website
- *Surfing* the Internet
- *Checking* email
- *Scrolling* down a page
- *Visiting* a site

All these actions are transient, fleeting.

In comparison, people *read* newspapers and magazines.

They *watch* TV.

Only if a magazine or program was particularly dull did anyone *flip* pages or *surf* channels.

By their very nature, the 'old' media are far more engaging. The distinct lack of engagement in online channels, however, is not due to any inherent problem with the media itself, and it certainly has nothing to do with the much-touted 'declining attention spans' of human beings.

It has everything to do with the utter lack of quality of the content—page after page, image after image, video after video, in the billions—that gets uploaded every day onto the cesspool of creative outpourings, a.k.a. the Internet.

Everyone with access to word processing software or a blog fancies themselves to be the next Charles Dickens.

Everyone with a phone camera, or camera phone, with more than six megapixels of resolution is an Ansel Adams.

And if the phone has HD video capabilities, the owner figures she or he may as well gun for an Oscar.

Not so long ago, reading business magazines was accepted, even recommended, at work. Today, ask any business owner what they think is the biggest drain on staff productivity. You already guessed the answer—social media.

While the lack of even a modicum of editorial intervention is responsible for the glut of drivel on the Internet, any attempt at control, or worse, censorship, defeats the whole purpose of the thing.

To those among us for whom communication is important, the solution is pretty much staring us in the face: *create better content.*

That admittedly is not easy. On the other hand, it is no harder today than it was in the days before the Internet.

Whatever we do, we can't blame the 'lack of time'.

The days haven't gotten shorter.

People don't have any *less* time on their hands than they did a hundred or even a thousand years ago. If anything, doing things has become easier.

Distracted by meaningless clutter and mindless goals, what we lack is a clue about *how to channel our precious moments towards a purpose that will render more meaning to our lives.* Communicators can, and indeed should, fill this void by creating content that genuinely addresses human aspirations.

# #18 DO YOU TRY TO TALK ABOVE THE NOISE?

In the 1980s, *The English Academy* at Chennai in South India was one of the places where the best spoken English was taught. The highlight of their public speaking course was an elocution competition where two speakers would speak on a topic—at the same time.

Quite a bit like the typical marketplace.

As the competition progressed, speakers were eliminated in round after round, and finally there were only two contestants left. The starting bell went off, and they launched into their speeches, full steam.

In seconds, the decibel levels had begun to rise. Soon it was a shouting match. Nobody in the audience could hear, much less understand, what either contestant said.

Finally one contestant ran out of words. The one who was left was declared the winner.

Then, the instructor stepped up to the plate and challenged the winner.

What followed was a lesson for every communicator in the world.

Once again, the winner blasted off, plunging into a tirade on his topic, scarcely pausing for breath.

On the other hand the teacher simply spoke, and did it calmly, slowly, and even *more softly* than his opponent. Not only did his soft voice cut through the noise, people listened and understood what he said.

So it is with any communication.

It is sufficient to say your piece. There's no need to yell and scream.

***

Like everything else, there are many ways of doing things, and some of them are the right ways.

There's no need to 'create urgency', as many marketing gurus advise. Making claims such as 'offer valid up to' or 'buy now' is gimmickry. If what we offer has value today, it had better have value tomorrow, and the day after, and next year, and the years after that.

Anyone with an ounce of wisdom sees right through such 'calls to action'—or CTAs as they are called—and ignores them.

Only scammers actively seek the audience of fools.

Is that really what we would like our personal and corporate brands to be?

More and more communications today talk in Maslow's terms—in other words, they push empowerment and self-actualization rather than fear or greed.

That is a good start.

The actual journey, however, is a bit longer.

Marketers and manufacturers alike need to think long and hard about how this empowerment *actually translates into real life.* Empowerment is a generic concept, and what a company says about it today can easily be replicated by another company tomorrow.

The difference, the erstwhile USP, is what the company *does* about empowerment.

Very often, the rubber never meets the road.

Another thing marketers need to do is relinquish the *urge to control.* Digital communication is a deluge. We sail against it at our own peril.

Many companies try to stem dissent by enforcing censorship, which reduces their corporate social media initiatives to an expensive and elaborate exercise in pointlessness.

Over the years, communication has become overly complicated. We have keywords, key phrases, search-ability, discover-ability, meta tags, and many other esoteric terms.

Yet communication remains what it always was—one person or a group of people saying something to other people.

The simpler we keep our communications, the more likely it is to succeed.

Ultimately there is only a very small set of core goals that people everywhere share.

The need for strong relationships.
The need to improve themselves.
The need to find fulfillment in all its many aspects.

Communicators need some serious soul-searching to figure out how we actually align with these goals—not create negative illusions based on sex and money as many used to, nor *positive illusions based on phony empowerment.*

With tons of channels: websites, micro sites, blogs, info-graphics, short films, online videos, podcasts, digital publications, newsletters, online resources, social media, mobile and wearable apps, and user-generated content, apart from conventional print, radio, film, TV, packaging, events, road shows, indoor and outdoor theme-based events, sculpture, installations, and street art—the list is endless—anyone seeking to communicate has no shortage of choices.

Rather than get confused by the clutter, individuals and companies need to get back to *the basics of communicating.*

If we keep flooding people's inboxes and mobile phones, they will tune out or simply leave.

# #19 ARTIFICIAL INTELLIGENCE OR NATURAL STUPIDITY?

In the early days of AI, scientists were struggling with a knotty problem: how to get a robot to cross a road safely.

As they monitored its progress remotely, they found it never even started to cross the road. They checked the entire electronic circuitry and found everything to be working fine. The mechanicals were also A-okay.

They tried again, and the robot still refused to budge.

Finally, they got back to the algorithm controlling it and discovered one line that essentially instructed the robot: *Do not cross the road if you see a vehicle.*

One of the scientists went to the empty road where the robot was being tested. That's when he noticed, some distance away, a parked vehicle.

He rushed back to the lab, and changed the program to instruct the robot: Do not cross the road if you see a *moving* vehicle.

They ran the test again.

It worked like a charm and the robot happily—to the extent robots are capable of happiness—crossed the road safely.

Beware what you tell a computer to do because that's exactly what it will do.

***

When the AI research company released the first version of a conversational generative pre-trained transformer, better known as ChatGPT, on 30 November 2022, they opened the doors to a journey that began several decades ago. The term "artificial intelligence" was coined in the 1950s by John McCarthy, an American computer scientist widely recognized as the "father of AI."

There are genuinely fantastic applications of AI, one of the most important being understanding the structure of protein molecules—the biggest challenge of a century. The use of AI models has been a game-changer in decoding these complex structures and can finally solve issues such as finding cures for diseases, disposing plastic waste, and minimizing climate change.

It seems pointless to discuss AI applications, agents, and models because they are evolving so rapidly that any information would surely be outdated in weeks. Broadly speaking, there are likely to be two new non-technical "job roles" that will emerge: junior AI collaborators and senior AI supervisors.

AI collaborators will use AI apps and agents to carry out their current work, except it will be about 100x faster. Meanwhile, AI supervisors will review AI-generated output through the lenses of accuracy, debiasing, confidentiality, and security. The best advice for digital content and marketing professionals would be to up their game by adding AI skills to their résumés.

Fortunately, this is not too hard to do. AI is rapidly becoming a buyer's market, with a plethora of apps and agents being made available for any given task, much like the mobile app boom of recent years.

A word about apps and agents: AI apps in their current form are simpler than agents. Apps perform straightforward tasks with some inputs from the user. Agents, on the other hand, can connect with external sources and complete end-to-end tasks autonomously. As an example, a holiday app can list out the pros and cons of various destinations, whereas a holiday agent will do all that and then go ahead and book a hotel room for the days you are free as well. That said, with the increasing sophistication of apps and the simultaneous simplification of agent interfaces, the distinguishing line between them is increasingly blurred. Soon enough, they may come to mean one and the same thing.

Like everything else, AI is not without bad actors and, because it is so powerful, can go sideways in spectacular ways that don't bode well for humanity. AI-controlled missile systems and war games come to mind. In fact, the "godfather of AI" and Nobel Prize winner, Geoffrey Hinton warned of the dangers of AI being misused as he stepped down from Google due to old age.

Starting a war is stupid. And if there's anything worse than natural stupidity, it's artificial stupidity.

# EPILOGUE

People as individuals, organizations, and communities are born for greatness, it is our destiny. The only worthy role of communication is to help as many as possible to achieve this goal by uncovering meaning and finding a purpose. The creation of wealth is one of the perks of life's journey and not its ultimate goal.

The economy exists to make people's lives better and *not the other way around.*

The economics of scale in production today consider only the financial aspect of market forces. When viewed through the wider lens of cultural, psychological, environmental, and social costs, it is often far from economical and, beyond a point, impossible to scale.

The adoption of a purely financial approach results in, *and cannot survive without,* the propagation of illusions to sustain a fundamentally faulty theory. *Maya* begins to set in before our pre-teens and rather than developing wholesome, integrated personalities, we end up with a society at odds with itself.

We have to deal with multiple personas—who people think we are, who we think we are, and who we really are.

Then, the interactions between people is reduced to a process of cutting through the conscious and unconscious smoke screens created by these personas, instead of a free, uninhibited, and symbiotic sharing of life experiences.

The main obstacle that we face is the lack of refinement and sensitivity of our consciousness that leads us to navigate our lives on this planet, much like driving a truck in a china shop. Overcoming this requires achieving a 'critical mass' of awareness amongst individuals and business entities.

Several organizations have come forward to embrace new ways of thinking. Known by different names, they all revolve around the concept of a 'circular economy' as a viable business proposition, rather than a token corporate sustainability initiative.(7)

To ensure that the entire planet embraces sustainable living only requires us to ask one question in all our communications: what is the future we want to create for coming generations?

# BIBLIOGRAPHY


1. **Sachs, Jonah.** *Winning the Story Wars.* Cambridge, MA : Harvard Business Review Press, 2012.

2. **Frommer, Dan.** *Most smartphone users download zero apps per month.* [Online] Quartz Media LLC, August 22, 2014. [Cited: September 24, 2016.] https://qz.com/253618/most-smartphone-users-download-zero-apps-per-month/.

3. **Ogilvy, David.** *Ogilvy & Mather.* [Online] Facebook. [Cited: September 24, 2016.] https://www.facebook.com/ogilvy/photos/pb.8106182993.-2207520000.1479636740./10154842265577994/.

4. **BBC.** *Glasgow hits Vegas jackpot.* [Online] BBC Scotland, March 7, 2000. [Cited: September 24, 2016.] http://news.bbc.co.uk/2/hi/uk_news/scotland/669007.stm.

5. **Aron, Jacob.** *Glassed-in DNA makes the ultimate time capsule.* [Online] New Scientist, February 11, 2015. [Cited: September 24, 2016.] https://www.newscientist.com/article/mg22530084-300-glassed-in-dna-makes-the-ultimate-time-capsule/#.VONYR1PF_Md.

6. **Vanhemert, Kyle.** *Watch: This Brilliant Lego Calendar Syncs With Google.* [Online] Wired, October 3, 2013. [Cited: September 24, 2016.] https://www.wired.

com/2013/10/a-brilliant-wall-mounted-lego-planner-that-syncs-with-google-calendar/.

7. **The Ellen MacArthur Foundation.** *Circular Economy.* [Online] [Cited: September 25, 2016.] https://www.ellenmacarthurfoundation.org/circular-economy/overview/concept.

# TERMINOLOGY

| | |
|---|---|
| ATF | Above The Fold refers to the part of a computer or mobile screen that is visible without scrolling |
| Bae | Short form of baby, a term of endearment |
| Below the fold | Below the fold refers to part of a computer or mobile screen that becomes visible only after the user scrolls down |
| Big idea | Some grand idea that forms the central theme of communication, a common term in advertising circles |
| Big value | The main, intrinsic benefit that a product offers the user |
| Bounce rate | The percentage of visitors who leave a website after viewing only one page, without interacting further |
| Brand loyalty | Preference for a particular product |
| Business model | A company's strategy for generating revenue and profits |
| CAC | Customer Acquisition Cost, which is the amount of money a company has to spend on advertising and promotion to get a customer |

| | |
|---|---|
| Channels | Ways to communicate to customers, such as magazines, newspapers, websites, social media, and mobile apps |
| CPC | Cost Per Click, which is the cost an advertiser pays for each click on their paid search ads |
| CTA | Call To Action refers to a prompt, usually a button, telling users to perform an action, like clicking a button or filling out a form |
| CTR | Click Through Rate is a measure of how often users click on your link compared to the number of times it appears in search engine results |
| Czar (also Tsar) | Title given to Russian emperors in the past |
| Czarina (also Tsarina) | Title given to Russian empresses in the past |
| Digital | Electronic system that uses 0's and 1's to collect, store, and transmit information |
| Digital garbage | Refers to the huge volume of digital content including text, images, audio, and video, that offer very little value to the user |
| Digital out of home (DOOH) | Digital Out Of Home refers to small or large-sized digital screens where promotional media is displayed in outdoor places |

| | |
|---|---|
| Digital poster | Electronic display of promotional material |
| Empowerment | Giving someone the power to make decisions, take actions, and gain control over their lives |
| Facepalm | Internet slang term referring to the act of putting one's palm on one's face out of sheer embarrassment, annoyance, or disappointment |
| Fleek | Flawless, especially referring to someone who is well-styled, groomed, or good-looking |
| Google Dance | Refers to major changes in keyword ranking in the search results within a short time |
| Grammar Nazi | Derogatory term for someone who always tries to correct errors in grammar, spelling, and punctuation in speech or writing |
| Hot zone (in a web page) | The triangular area in the top left of a web page which first gets the readers' attention |
| Influencer | Individuals who have a large number of social media followers and can influence their opinion, especially in areas like fashion, fitness, travel, and food |
| LTV | Lifetime Value is an estimate of the total revenue a business can expect from a customer in their lifetime |

| | |
|---|---|
| Lyk | Internet slang for Let You Know |
| Marketplace | In the digital world, a platform where buyers and sellers connect |
| Maya | Sanskrit word for "illusion" that usually refers to the temporary, material world |
| Media | Channels of communication including newspapers, magazines, TV, mobile, websites, and social media |
| Organic search results | Listings that appear on search engine results pages, which are not paid-for or sponsored |
| Out of home (OOH) | Out Of Home refers to small or large-sized screens where promotional media is displayed in outdoor places |
| Paid search | Digital marketing strategy in which businesses pay to display their ads on search engine results pages |
| Panda algorithm | Search engine update introduced by Google in 2011 to give higher ranking to websites with high-quality content |
| PPA | Pay Per Action refers to the amount paid every time the user performs an action, e.g., download |
| PPC | Pay Per Click refers to the amount paid every time the user clicks a link, usually an advertisement or banner |

| | |
|---|---|
| Search results | List of webpages that appear when the user searches for a keyword or phrase |
| SEM | Search Engine Marketing is the paid promotion of a website in search engine results |
| SEO | Search Engine Optimization refers to improving website content and navigation quality to increase the number of visitors |
| SMM | Social Media Marketing refers to usage of social media to build brands or sell products |
| SERP | Search Engine Results Page is the list of webpages that appear when the user searches for a keyword or phrase |
| Site authority | Website's overall ranking in the search engine |
| Skip | Refers to the action of clicking next without viewing a webpage, video, or mobile screen |
| Smart watch | High-tech watch that can perform actions like handling phone calls, monitoring pulse rate, counting steps walked by the user, and more |
| Social media | Channels where people can connect and exchange ideas and information |

| | |
|---|---|
| Solus | The bottom right quarter in the front page of a newspaper where the most expensive ads are displayed |
| Spam | Unwanted communication, usually emails or messages |
| Stop press | Refers to late news or headlines usually inserted in newspapers at the last minute |
| Swipe | Sliding a finger across a mobile app screen, usually left for dislike and right for like |
| Turnt | Slang for extremely excited or intoxicated |
| U R D 1 4 me | Slang for You Are The One For Me |
| Wearable | Electronic devices that can be worn on the body, e.g., smart watches and fitness trackers |
| Website banners | Digital advertisements for products or services appearing on a website |
| YMMV | Short form of Your Mileage May Vary, which means different users can get different results while doing the same thing |